The Importance of the Parables of Jesus

You might be wondering why are the Parables of Jesus important?

They teach important moral and spiritual lessons. The Parables of Jesus use simple stories and everyday situations to teach children important moral and spiritual lessons that they can apply to their daily lives. Through these stories, children can learn about virtues such as kindness, forgiveness, and love.

They help children understand the teachings of Jesus: The Parables of Jesus are a way for children to understand the teachings of Jesus in a way that is accessible to them. By using stories that are relatable to children, Jesus was able to explain complex spiritual concepts in a way that was easy for them to understand.

They promote critical thinking and reflection: The Parables of Jesus are not straightforward stories with clear-cut answers. Instead, they require children to think critically and reflect on their meaning. This encourages children to develop their analytical and reasoning skills, which can benefit them in all areas of their lives.

They foster a love of reading and learning: The Parables of Jesus are engaging and entertaining stories that can foster a love of reading and learning in children. By introducing children to the stories of Jesus at an early age, parents and educators can instill a lifelong love of reading and learning in them.

Overall, the Parables of Jesus are an important part of Christian education for children. They provide a powerful tool for parents and educators to teach children about important spiritual concepts and to encourage them to live virtuous lives.

Parable of the Speck and the Log

The Parable of the Speck and the Log is a story that Jesus told to teach us about the importance of not judging other people.

One day, Jesus said, Why do you look at the speck of sawdust in your brother's eye and pay no attention to the plank in your own eye? How can you say to your brother, 'Let me take the speck out of your eye,' when all the time there is a plank in your own eye?

You hypocrite, first take the
plank out of your own eye,
and then you will see clearly
to remove the speck from
your brother's eye.

What does this story mean? Well, imagine that your friend has a tiny piece of sawdust in their eye. It might hurt them and make it hard for them to see. You want to help them, so you go over to them and try to get the speck out.

But what if you had a big log in your own eye? You wouldn't even be able to see your friend properly, let alone help them with their problem. So, before you can help your friend, you need to take the log out of your own eye first.

In the same way, Jesus was telling us that we shouldn't judge other people for their faults and problems when we have our own faults and problems to deal with. We need to take care of our own problems first before we can help others.

So, the lesson we can learn from the Parable of the Speck and the Log is that we should always try to be understanding and kind to others, and not judge them for their faults and mistakes, because we all have our own faults and mistakes too.

The Parable of New Cloth on Old Garment

The Parable of New Cloth on Old Garment is a story that Jesus told to teach us about the importance of being careful when making changes in our lives.

One day, Jesus said, "No one sews a patch of new cloth on an old garment, for the patch will pull away from the garment, making the tear worse."

What does this story mean? Well, imagine that you have a favorite old shirt that you love to wear. It's been through a lot with you, and it has some holes in it. You want to fix it, so you get some new cloth and sew it over the holes.

But what if the new cloth is too thick or too strong for the old shirt? As you wear the shirt and move around, the new cloth might start to pull away from the old shirt, making the holes even worse than before.

In the same way, Jesus was telling us that we need to be careful when we try to make changes in our lives. Just like the new cloth and old shirt, sometimes the changes we make might not work well together. We need to think carefully and make sure that the changes we make are the right ones for us.

The lesson we can learn from the Parable of New Cloth on Old Garment is that we need to be thoughtful and careful when we make changes in our lives. We should take the time to think about what we want to change, and how we can make those changes in a way that works well with who we are and what we want to do.

The Parable of the Divided Kingdom

The Parable of the Divided Kingdom is a story that Jesus told to teach us about the importance of unity and working together.

One day, Jesus said, "Every kingdom divided against itself will be ruined, and every city or household divided against itself will not stand."

What does this story mean? Well, imagine that you and your friends are building a sandcastle at the beach. You all have different ideas about how the castle should look, and you start to argue about it.

Some of you want to build a big tower, while others want to make a moat. Pretty soon, you're all arguing so much that you're not getting anything done.

In the same way, Jesus was telling us that when we don't work together and instead fight and argue, we can't accomplish anything. We need to work together and be united to accomplish our goals.

So, the lesson we can learn from the Parable of the Divided Kingdom is that it's important to work together and be united, whether it's in our families, our schools, or our communities. When we work together, we can accomplish great things, but when we're divided, we can't accomplish anything.

The Parable of The Sower

The Parable of the Sower is a story that Jesus told to teach us about how different people respond to the word of God.

One day, Jesus said, "A farmer went out to sow his seed. As he was scattering the seed, some fell along the path, and the birds came and ate it up. Some fell on rocky places, where it did not have much soil. It sprang up quickly because the soil was shallow. But when the sun came up, the plants were scorched, and they withered because they had no root."

"Other seed fell among thorns, which grew up and choked the plants. Still, other seed fell on good soil, where it produced a crop—a hundred, sixty, or thirty times what was sown."

What does this story mean? Well, imagine that you want to plant a garden in your backyard. You get some seeds and start to plant them. Some of the seeds fall on the sidewalk, where they can't grow.

Some of the seeds fall on rocky ground, where they grow quickly but can't get enough water. Some of the seeds fall among weeds, which grow up and choke the plants. But some of the seeds fall on good soil, where they can grow strong and produce a lot of vegetables.

In the same way, Jesus was telling us that when we hear the word of God, we can respond in different ways. Some people might hear the word of God but not understand it or ignore it. Other people might hear the word of God and get excited about it, but then give up when things get tough.

Still, others might hear the word of God, but let other things in life distract them from following it. But some people hear the word of God and understand it, and they let it grow in their hearts, making them strong and fruitful.

The lesson we can learn from the Parable of the Sower is that we need to be like the good soil, where the word of God can take root and grow strong in our hearts. We should try to understand the word of God and let it guide us in our lives, so we can be strong and fruitful, like a good garden.

The Parable of the Two Sons

The Parable of the Two Sons is a story that Jesus told to teach us about the importance of obedience.

One day, Jesus said, "There was a man who had two sons. He went to the first and said, 'Son, go and work today in the vineyard.' 'I will not,' he answered, but later he changed his mind and went. Then the father went to the other son and said the same thing. He answered, 'I will, sir,' but he did not go.

What does this story mean? Well, imagine that your parents ask you to clean your room. The first time they ask, you might say, "No, I don't want to do it." But later, you might change your mind and clean your room anyway. The second time your parents ask, you might say, "Yes, I'll do it right away!" but then you might get distracted and not do it at all.

In the same way, Jesus was telling us that it's not enough just to say that we'll do something. We need to actually do it. The son who said he wouldn't work in the vineyard but then changed his mind and did it anyway was better than the son who said he would work in the vineyard but then didn't do it.

The lesson we can learn from the Parable of the Two Sons is that it's important to obey our parents and do what they ask us to do, even if we don't want to at first. We should always try to follow through on our promises and be obedient, just like the son who changed his mind and did the work in the vineyard.

Made in the USA
Monee, IL
30 August 2024

64969508R00046